The Know It All Book of Peace

Waldo Rochow, MBA

Published by the author
Edited by Will Rochow
Cover by Waldo Rochow
    with elements of *The portal* by: pualv (www.flickr.com/photos/8460740@N05)
    CC-BY 2.0 (accessed: 27 Jul 2014)

Website: http:// know-it-all.rochow.info

ISBN: 978-1-926469-01-0

Volume #24 in the ***Know It All*** series:

The Know It All Book of Astronomy
The Know It All Book of Biology
The Know It All Book of Business
The Know It All Book of Chemistry
The Know It All Book of Climate Change
The Know It All Book of Conservation
The Know It All Book of Economics
The Know It All Book of Education
The Know It All Book of Equality
The Know It All Book of Gastronomy
The Know It All Book of Geology
The Know It All Book of Geopolitics
The Know It All Book of Health Care
The Know It All Book of History
The Know It All Book of Justice

The Know It All Book of Leadership
The Know It All Book of Literature
The Know It All Book of Marketing
The Know It All Book of Mathematics
The Know It All Book of Meteorology
The Know It All Book of Music
The Know It All Book of Oceanography
The Know It All Book of Oenology
The Know It All Book of Peace
The Know It All Book of Physics
The Know It All Book of Politics
The Know It All Book of Poverty
The Know It All Book of Psychiatry
The Know It All Book of Technology
The Know It All Book of Theology

To my loving wife Joanne, for putting up
with my silly side all these years;

To my sons Karl and Paul, for following in
my silly shoes;

To my parents, for instilling in all your kids
and grandkids an appreciation for the silly
side of life;

To my brother Will, for your tireless editing
support; and

To all the people of the world, for giving me
something to laugh about.

Thank you for joining me on this journey. The purpose of this book is actually deeper than its tongue-in-cheek treatment here suggests. While on the surface it might appear that I am scoffing at higher learning, nothing could be further from the truth. It is my goal to encourage the reader to think, and study, and to not be satisfied with the status quo. In fact, I would be thrilled if you fill this book with your own observations.

As someone with an interest in this subject, why shouldn't you write *The Book of Knowledge*? You just might be seen by future generations as the *Father* or *Mother* of the study of Peace. Sure, you won't be the first author on the subject (after all, neither was I), but you could be the most significant.

I hope that you will become a contagion of inquisitiveness. Be that gal or that guy that is constantly asking *why*. Contaminate your friends and family with curiosity. Consider the possibility that much, if not all, that we know today on any subject may be completely wrong. Challenge the assumptions upon which your knowledge is based.

You just might be surprised what you can still learn after you
know it all.

-- Waldo Rochow, MBA